FIRST IMPRESSIONS

JOHN JAMES AUDUBON

JOSEPH KASTNER

Harry N. Abrams, Inc., Publishers, New York

SERIES EDITOR: Robert Morton
EDITOR: Ellyn Childs Allison
DESIGNER: Joan Lockhart
PICTURE RESEARCH: Neil Ryder Hoos

Library of Congress Cataloging-in-Publication Data
Kastner, Joseph.
John James Audubon / Joseph Kastner.
p. cm. — (First impressions)
Includes index.
Summary: Examines the noted artist whose passion for
American birds dominated his life and his work.
ISBN 0-8109-1918-4
1. Audubon, John James, 1785–1851— Juvenile literature.
2. Ornithologists—United States—Biography—Juvenile
literature. 3. Animal painters—United States—Biography—
Juvenile literature [1. Audubon, John James, 1785–1851.
2. Naturalists. 3. Artists.]
I. Title. II. Series: First impressions (New York, N.Y.).
QL31.A9K37 1992
598'.092—dc20   91–44659
CIP
AC

Printed and bound
in Hong Kong

Chapter One

{ornamental divider}

BIRDS AND DESTINY

Audubon's two sons, Victor and John Wood-house, honored their aging father in 1848 in a joint portrait of him as the frontier naturalist he once had been.

t is a spring morning in 1795 in the village of Couëron in western France and Jean Jacques Audubon, a handsome boy of ten with an easy smile, picks up his lunch basket, puts a pad and pencil in his pocket, and heads for the countryside. Crawling into the hedgerows, he finds birds sitting in their nests and lifts out a few eggs. A wild duck flies up from the reeds and Jean makes a quick sketch.

It is early on a summer day on the Kentucky frontier in 1815. Audubon walks out from behind the counter of the general store he owns in Henderson and heads out into the forest. He wears a fringed buckskin jacket and carries a gun and sketch pad. A loud rapping noise leads him to a redheaded woodpecker hammering at a branch. Pencil quickly in hand, he sketches the bird's movements. He comes home pleased, with a pad full of drawings and the partridges he has shot for dinner. Meanwhile, a clerk has been taking care of the business at the store.

It is a July morning in 1819 on a road outside Henderson. Audubon, his clothes dusty and his face despondent, is trudging along, not looking back at the store he has been forced to sell. He has no eyes or ears now for birds. They are his enemies, he says to himself. They have brought him to failure and bankruptcy. He wishes they had never existed.

Of course he didn't really mean that—and he knew it. Only a year later he was on a flatboat going down the Mississippi with a batch of bird drawings, barely enough money to pay his fare, and an enormous task before him. From now on, he would give everything else up in order to paint all the birds of America. With a newly found will and an astonishing burst of genius, John James Audubon made himself the most famous painter of birds the world has ever known.

Chapter Two

TO THE
NEW
WORLD

Audubon always remembered that day in 1796 when his father, a sea captain, came home on one of his infrequent visits. What had he been up to? the captain asked his son. Proudly Jean showed his collections of birds' nests and plants.

The captain, who encouraged the boy's interest in nature, was pleased. "And your schoolwork?" he asked. Jean hesitated, then confessed he had hardly opened a book. That evening the captain asked Jean to play something on his violin. Shamefaced, the boy brought out the instrument. Its strings were broken and the unused bow was dusty.

Captain Audubon, his son had come to know, had a fierce temper— "like the blast of a hurricane." This time, to Jean's surprise and relief, he just hummed a little tune to himself and sent the boy off to bed.

Jean admired his father, a strict but loving man who hoped his son would become an officer in the French Navy as he himself had been, fighting in two wars against the British. Jean never knew his mother. Between wars, the captain had bought a sugar plantation in Sainte-Domingue (later Haiti) in the West Indies, and though he had a wife in France, he installed a young Frenchwoman as mistress of the plantation. On April 26, 1785, she gave birth to a son, Jean Jacques. She died while the boy was still an infant. A few years later the captain brought his son to France, where Madame Audubon, who had no children of her own,

"A graceful country seat," Audubon called his boyhood home, La Gerbetière, in western France near the Loire River. He spent his days in the fields and marshes watching and drawing birds.

took Jean into her heart as if he had been her own son. She was, perhaps, too loving, for she let him neglect his schoolwork, hiding his faults from her husband.

But on the evening when Captain Audubon learned of Jean's unopened schoolbooks and saw the broken violin, those faults could not be hidden any longer. The next morning Jean Jacques was shaken awake very early and, his trunk already packed, was bundled into a horse-drawn coach. For three days, Captain Audubon read his book, speaking hardly a word to his son until their carriage clattered into the port of Rochefort. Here we are, the captain said and enrolled Jean in the navy's training school.

When he came to America in 1803, Audubon lived at Mill Grove in Pennsylvania. (seen here and on page 13). His father had bought the place hoping to mine its deposits of lead. A smelting mill was built but did not prove profitable. The estate today is an Audubon museum.

In climbing masts and setting sails or in swimming and shooting, Jean was outstanding—but not in his nautical studies. After three and a half years, he flunked his mathematics tests and Captain Audubon reluctantly took him out of the navy.

Jean was not unhappy to be home. He had to go back to school and work at his music lessons. But he also took dancing and fencing lessons and, best of all, had plenty of time for birds. He worked over his drawings but they weren't very good. "Stiff, unmeaning profiles," he himself later called them. Still, he kept trying. His father wondered what to do with him.

Some years before, the captain had put some money into a farm at Mill Grove in Pennsylvania, not far from Philadelphia. If Jean were given some responsibility, he thought, he might settle into a career. Besides, Napoleon was conscripting young men for his armies and the captain wanted to save his son from that. He came to a decision: Jean would go to America and learn to manage Mill Grove.

So in 1803, at the age of eighteen, Jean Jacques Audubon came to live in a nation that was not quite ten years older than he was.

A comfortable place, Audubon decided when he got to Mill Grove, and not much like Couëron. Things were bigger and wilder. The roomy stone house sat on a hill looking over farmland and orchards that ran into forests thicker than those he knew in France. The terrain was rougher, especially where a creek had cut caves and a deep ravine into ledges of rock. Soon he was out exploring, listening to unfamiliar bird songs and filling his pads with sketches of birds whose names he didn't know.

Mill Grove, he found out, was running along very well, with a farmer who worked the land and an agent who managed its business. The arrangement suited Audubon. Responsibility was nothing he cared to take on. He acted, as he himself later wrote, "with as little concern about the future as if the world had been made for me. Hunting, fishing, drawing, and music occupied my every moment." Brought up to be a gentleman, he let others attend to the chores at Mill Grove while he took on a gentleman's social life. "Not a ball, a skating match or a house or riding party took place without me," he said.

His new friends found him carefree to the point of recklessness. Out skating with them one afternoon, he raced heedlessly ahead and, before anyone could warn him, plunged through a hole and disappeared. Skating frantically after him, his companions came to another hole, and there was Jean holding onto the edge of the ice. Another time, challenging Jean's marksmanship, a friend tossed his cap into the air as Jean came skating by, carrying his gun. Without slackening speed, Jean raised the gun and fired, and the cap came down as full of holes as a sieve.

Here, as in France, he collected almost everything he could find in nature. The walls of his room were festooned with birds' eggs, carefully blown out and strung upon thread. The fireplace mantel was covered with stuffed squirrels, raccoons, and opossums. The shelves were filled with fish, frogs, snakes, and lizards. And on the walls hung dozens of his bird drawings.

Everyone welcomed the young Frenchman's company. He had grown into a slim, handsome man, about five feet ten inches tall, with a charming air and a look of wiry strength. His face was lively and his eyes a hazel color. His nose had an aristocratic sharpness, his long hair was a glossy brown. Both his mind and his hands were quick. His conversation was amusing and so were the sleight-of-hand tricks he liked to show off.

One thing could take Jean away from his social life. He had fallen in love with America's birds. In a cave on a creek that ran through the farm,

he spent days watching a family of phoebes, small gray birds that get their name from their song—*fee-bee, fee-bee, fee-bee.* As they darted through the air chasing insects, they seemed to him to be full of gaiety and engaged in the most interesting conversations.

The phoebes did not welcome him at first, flying swiftly at him and snapping their bills sharply. But before a week had passed, the birds got used to their watcher and would, he wrote, "come close by me as if I had been a post." Taking a transparent white egg out of a nest, he felt he was handling something "more precious than diamonds." When the phoebes hatched, he gently lifted out the fledglings, which would, without protest, let him hold them.

What would happen, he wondered, after the young birds grew up and left? Would they come back to the cave next year? Devising his own way of finding out, he tied fine silver threads around their legs, loosely enough not to hurt but so fastened that the bird could not remove them. If they did return, he would know them by these threads. In this simple experiment, he was far ahead of his time, anticipating a method now called banding. Modern ornithologists, the scientists who study birds, trap birds in nets and fasten tiny tags to their legs, noting on them the place and time the bird was tagged. If the birds are caught again, the tags will tell how they have traveled, enabling ornithologists to track migrating birds and understand their habits.

Studying all aspects of bird life, Audubon made drawings of their eggs. He planned to include these in *The Birds of America,* but finally decided not to.

Sure enough, next spring Audubon saw two phoebes with those tiny threads still on their legs. Later he came upon a pair of phoebes nesting near the caves. One flew off but the other let him get very close, and he decided that this was one of the birds he used to pick up and hold in his hand. He knew now that phoebes came back year after year to the same place to nest.

He kept on drawing birds but when he looked at his sketches, he would shake his head. His creatures had no real life in them, and they certainly could never fly. He tried making a model out of cork and wire. "A grotesque dodo," he told himself and kicked it into pieces. Then one morning he woke with an inspiration.

Ignoring breakfast, he rode into town, bought some wire, went out and shot a kingfisher, and set to work. He pierced the body, fixed it to a board with a wire, passed a second wire around the upper part of the

beak to hold the head up and with finer wires arranged the feet. The last wire, he wrote, "delightfully elevated the tail and at last—there stood before me a real kingfisher. I outlined the bird with the aid of compasses, then colored and finished it. That was my first drawing actually from nature, for even the model's eye was still as if full of life."

Then he fell in love again, this time with a tall, dark-haired girl named Lucy Bakewell, who lived on a neighboring farm. Shortly after Audubon had arrived at Mill Grove, Lucy's father paid a call on his new neighbor. Not finding him at home, Mr. Bakewell left his card. Audubon did not return the call, possibly because he was forgetful but perhaps for another reason. Because his father had fought against the English,

Captain Audubon had come to hate them, and his son shared some of his feelings. "I wish to know none of that race," he declared.

He lost some of those feelings when he met Mr. Bakewell while out hunting and found him a warm and pleasant man. Jean said he was sorry for not having returned the call. No need to apologize, said Mr. Bakewell and invited Jean to lunch. Lucy was sitting in the parlor when he arrived, and she asked him to join her. While she sewed, she talked to him, "to make the time pleasant for me," he thought. When she stood up to go to lunch, "her form showed both grace and beauty," he told his sons years later. "My heart followed every one of her steps."

Lucy was an unusual young woman. In a time when most parents brought up their daughters simply to make a good marriage, the Bakewells gave Lucy what would be today a college-level education. She read the books in their large library, guided by her father and by her mother, who was related to the famous English writer Samuel Johnson. In their home in England, she had met scientists and writers, including Erasmus Darwin, whose grandson Charles Darwin formulated the theory of evolution. Lucy grew up to have a mind of her own. She thought clearly, expressed herself directly, and helped manage the household efficiently.

Soon Jean was spending as much time at the Bakewells' plantation as at Mill Grove. At first Lucy's parents were doubtful. He would come courting with his hair hanging down to his shoulders. His English accent was odd and his grammar peculiar. Besides, he was not tending to his duties at Mill Grove. But Lucy was drawn to him, flattered—despite her good sense—to have this dashing, different young Frenchman as a suitor. She improved his English and he taught her French. When he played the violin, she accompanied him on the piano. She read her books to him and he showed her his birds. Feeling at home in America, he began to call himself John James instead of Jean Jacques.

Much as he liked Audubon, Mr. Bakewell looked on him as too

young and too useless to be married and sent Lucy off to New York to forget him. Of course she didn't. John called on Mrs. Bakewell daily on one excuse or another, and often found there was a message from Lucy. Finally Mr. Bakewell gave in to his daughter's wishes and agreed that they could marry.

John went back to France to convince his father of what he called "the prudency of my choice." His stay there had a significance he realized only years later. A young naturalist named Charles D'Orbigny took John out on instructive bird walks, and in this casual way John was given a grounding in ornithology, adding scientific knowledge to what he had taught himself. His drawings of birds showed that he had a developing eye for their characteristics; he could also give them a certain charm, as can be seen in his sketch on page 18.

Captain Audubon deliberated and then gave his consent to the marriage. Since John had done little at Mill Grove, the captain had arranged a business partnership between him and Ferdinand Rozier, the son of a friend. The two young men sailed for America to set up as storekeepers and merchants in the newly opening west.

Audubon carried the good news to Lucy and her father. Lucy's uncle in New York arranged to give him some experience in business by taking him on as an apprentice. John got off to a shaky start by mailing a letter containing $8,000 in currency and forgetting to seal the envelope. Happily, it was delivered intact. He was up early every morning, not because he was eager to get to work but because he wanted to stop at the big markets to make sketches of the wild ducks and game birds that were for sale. Something inside him must have told him what would be most important to him some day. He took time off to help a naturalist named Samuel Latham Mitchill stuff and preserve bird and animal specimens.

Dr. Mitchill introduced Audubon not only to the study of natural history but also to the odd and wonderful men who were attracted to that science. The doctor himself seemed to know and do almost everything. He practiced medicine, taught botany and chemistry at

Audubon's Shearwater. 1826.

On this sketch of a bird later named after him, Audubon

noted its total length, general coloration ("sooty black above, snowy

white below") and the color of its nails ("blue black"),

eyelids ("light blue") and eyes ("dark blue nearly black").

Columbia College, deciphered Babylonian cuneiform, collected Fiji costumes, and was an authority on American fish. In the United States Congress, where he served as representative and later as senator, he was called, because of his long speeches on almost every subject, "a living encyclopedia" and sometimes "a chaos of knowledge." Dr. Mitchill gave his young helper a good grounding in taxidermy (preserving specimens) and animal anatomy and physiology.

An unfortunate misunderstanding ended his instructions. Neighbors of the apartment Dr. Mitchill used as his laboratory were alarmed by the strong smell of formaldehyde that came from the rooms. Formaldehyde is the chemical used in embalming corpses, and the neighbors imparted their dark suspicions to the police. A constable came to investigate and discovered that what Audubon was embalming were only birds and fish. That was innocent enough, the constable admitted, but it would have to stop.

Saying goodbye for a while to Lucy, Audubon went out with Rozier to Louisville, Kentucky, then a town of a thousand inhabitants. Renting a store, they stocked it with goods they had brought. Frontier stores in those days sold almost everything a family might need—flour, sugar, salt, calico, wool clothes, guns and gunpowder pouches, spades and saws, axes and needles, whiskey and wine, tobacco and coffee, books and music boxes. Leaving Rozier in charge, Audubon went back to Pennsylvania to claim Lucy.

They were married on a gusty April day in 1808 at Lucy's home, in the parlor where they had first met. Three days later, as so many adventurous men were doing then, John took his bride west.

Chapter Three

ON
THE
FRONTIER

It was a grueling journey for Lucy. Their stagecoach bumped and rocked over the crude roads, barely able to make it up the steep mountains and speeding out of control down the slopes. Once it turned over and, with Lucy flung around inside, the coach was dragged hundreds of yards before the frightened horses could be stopped. She crawled out badly bruised.

Brought up in a home of refinement, Lucy was plunged into the rough, coarse life of the American frontier. At crowded inns along the road, the Audubons had to share their bug-ridden beds with other travelers. There was "no dearth of bedfellows and insects," Lucy bravely wrote her sisters. Drunken travelers kept her awake with their quarrelsome card games, their drunken roistering, and their bloody fights.

Things went somewhat better when they transferred to a boat and went down the Ohio River. Lucy delighted in the springtime flowers she could pick along the banks and, like John, found excitement in the wildness that was everywhere. They were young, of course.

So was the country they were coming into. The roads and the rivers were filled with men and women and children eager to make new lives for themselves in a place where the towns were only dirt streets and log buildings, where the wilderness started at the edge of the last farm and stretched endlessly across the Louisiana Territory that the United States

When he was in London later in his life, Audubon poked fun

at his custom of wearing frontier garb by drawing this caricature

of himself as the "American Woodsman".

had just bought from France.

For Audubon, it was as different a world from Mill Grove as Mill Grove had been from France. All through his life he was able to fit in wherever he was. Now he became a man of the frontier, and the vitality he took from it would one day lend greatness to his art.

Landing at Louisville, the Audubons took up lodgings in an inn called the Indian Queen. Then, at last, John James settled down to business. Except that he never really settled down.

There was too much else to do and see and learn. It was still the land of pioneers and of the heroes who had opened the West. The Revolutionary general George Rogers Clark told Audubon stories about his great victories over the British and Indian forces. The general's brother William, who had been a leader of the famous Lewis and Clark expedition into the Louisiana Territory, told Audubon about the birds he had observed on their explorations.

Audubon made friends with the Indians and, as everybody always did, they enjoyed his company. At night around the Shawnee campfires he would take out the fiddle that he liked to carry with him and play dance tunes for them. The squaws, he remembered, "laughed heartily at the merriment." In return, the Shawnees helped make their fiddler a man of the wilderness, teaching him how to hunt bear, how to fish through the ice, how to find his way through the vast forests. He became a true woodsman, able and unafraid to travel for days at a time with only his dog for company, shooting or catching his dinners and bedding down when he had to in the shelter of thickets.

On one long winter trip, he came at nightfall to a settler's cabin and asked the woman inside if he might sleep there. She said yes, and upon entering he found a young Indian brave with a bloodied, empty eye socket—the eyeball had been gouged out in an accident and he, like Audubon, had sought shelter. Taking out his gold watch, Audubon remarked to the woman that it was late and he was tired. "She spied my watch covetously," his story goes, and "to gratify her curiosity I passed it to her. She was all ecstasy and put the chain round her brawny neck."

Audubon thought nothing of it until the Indian walked past him, pinched him and, with his one good eye, gave him a look "so forbidding that it struck a chill within me." Realizing that the Indian was warning him of some danger, Audubon drew his gun close to his body as he lay down on some bearskins and feigned sleep.

In a little while, the woman's two sons entered and helped themselves freely to whiskey. As they drew into a corner to talk, Audubon heard the woman mention his watch. "I saw her take a large carving knife and, like the incarnate fiend she was, whet its edge at the grindstone. Turning to her reeling sons she said, 'There, that will soon settle him. Boys kill yon—, and then for the watch!'

"I turned and cocked my gun-locks silently, touched my faithful dog, and lay ready to start up and shoot the first comer. The infernal hag slowly advanced. That night might have been my last in this world had Providence not started a rescue. The door opened. Two stout travelers walked in, each with a long rifle on his shoulder. I bounced to my feet. In a minute the tale was told."

They tied up the drunken sons along with their mother while "the

Indian fairly danced for joy." At daylight, dealing out frontier justice, they set fire to the cabin, gave the skins and implements to the young Indian warric and went on their way.

Audubon's horse, Barro, shared his master's adventures. A half-tamed mustang, Barro was offered to Audubon by a trader who had bought him from the Osage Indians. "Not a handsome animal," Audubon noted, as he looked over the horse. His large head bulged out in front, his thick mane was unkempt, and his scanty tail almost dragged along the ground. But he had a broad chest and there was spirit in his eyes. When Audubon tried him out, Barro jumped over a huge log "as lightly as an elk." In a muddy swamp he kept his nose close to the water, "as if to judge of its depth with a caution that pleased me." Swimming across the Ohio River, he breathed freely "and without the grunting noises made by many horses."

So Audubon bought Barro, who became so attached to his master that he was allowed to graze free instead of being tethered at night and, no matter how thirsty he was, he would not drink water until Audubon told him to.

Chimney Swift. **1824.**

In Kentucky, Audubon came on a huge sycamore tree whose hollow trunk housed thousands of chimney swifts—nine thousand, he calculated. He drew two nests, one of them clinging to the tree.

On one of his journeys Audubon met a gentleman named Vincent Nolte, who was mounted on a superb horse which, he told Audubon, cost him three hundred dollars. Audubon praised the horse and Nolte said, not very courteously, that he wished Audubon's was as good. Audubon ignored the snub and politely asked when Nolte expected to reach his destination for that night. "Just soon enough to have some trout ready for our supper," Nolte replied, "if you will join me when you get there."

Barro, his master felt, seemed to understand the conversation. When Nolte put his horse into a quick trot, Barro pricked up his ears, lengthened his pace, and pulled away. By the time Nolte arrived at the inn, Audubon was standing in the doorway announcing that he had ordered trout for their dinner.

Sometime later, Audubon and Barro were riding near the Mississippi River when, Audubon related, "a sudden strange darkness rose from the western horizon. I heard a distant rumbling and spurred my steed into a gallop. The animal, however, knew better than I what was coming. He nearly stopped and put one foot down after another with such measured caution that he might have been walking on ice. All of a sudden, he began a piteous groaning, hung his head, spread his four legs to brace himself and stood stock still. I would have sprung from his back had not all the trees and shrubs begun to sway from their roots. The ground rose and fell in billows like the ruffled waters of a

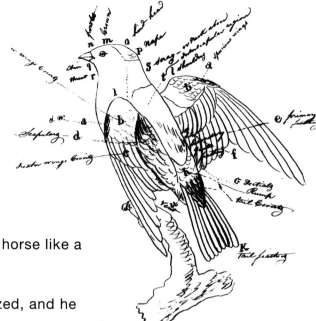

lake. I found myself rocking on my horse like a child in a cradle."

An earthquake! Audubon realized, and he expected the "ground to open up and reveal an abyss to engulf me. The fearful convulsion lasted only minutes. Barro drew up, raised his head and galloped off, as if frolicking without a rider."

It was a close call. The great earthquake of 1811–12 was the worst ever known to hit the Midwest. For months, the earth shook in a series of tremors. Riverbanks caved in, islands disappeared, and, for a short while as the ground heaved, the Mississippi River ran backward.

The frontiersmen who became Audubon's friends loved practical jokes, and Audubon did too—and had no shame in telling about them. He was out riding once with a visitor from Europe when they "spied a beautiful black and pale yellow animal with a bushy tail.

"' Mr. Audubon,' the visitor exclaimed, 'isn't that a beautiful squirrel?'

"'Yes,' Audubon answered, 'and of a kind that will let you approach and lay hold of it.' "

The visitor took up a stick and whacked the animal, which "raised its fine tail and let fire." The "squirrel" was, of course, a skunk and the visitor could not get the smell out of his coat for days. "I can still laugh almost as heartily as I did then," wrote Audubon.

Wherever he went on his journeys, Audubon carried his pad and pencil to draw birds, his gun to shoot specimens, and his ornithology books to help identify and classify the birds he saw. Most of them were not in his books, which were written by Europeans. They gave him little information about American birds and he found much of it inaccurate. The only way he could learn what he wanted to know was to teach himself, and he did so not just by watching and drawing but by measuring and dissecting, studying nests and eggs, and recording the birds' habits.

His methodical investigation of the local chimney swifts showed how businesslike he could be. The swifts, a species of swallow, roosted for the night in a large, hollow sycamore tree. Putting his ear to the trunk, Audubon could hear a "roaring noise made within by the birds . . . like the sound of a large waterwheel revolving under a powerful stream." He cut a large hole in the tree, squeezed inside, and counted the number of birds crowded on one square foot of the trunk. Multiplying this by the number of square feet in the trunk, he concluded that there were nine thousand swallows packed into the one tree. What is most interesting about the study was not so much the figure he came up with as his curiosity about it and the pains he took to get it.

By patient watching, he learned how the snowy owl in winter caught its food. It lay flat on the river ice, he wrote, "with its head down near the water. One might have supposed the bird sound asleep. The instant a fish rose to the surface, the owl thrust out the claw that was next to the water and drew it out like lightning."

As he came to know birds better, his feeling for them deepened. Wading out into the Wabash River, he approached the nest of an avocet, a water bird with a long, curved beak. The bird was sitting on her nest. "I crawled within three feet. Her head was almost mournfully sunk among her plumage, her eyes were half closed as if she were dreaming. Now she observes me, poor thing. Off she scrambles, running, tumbling, and rising on the clicking notes of grief and anxiety."

On a March morning in 1810, another of those extraordinary men who inhabited the world of natural history walked into Audubon's life— and changed it forever. Working in his store, Audubon looked up from the counter to see a lean, sad-faced traveler enter carrying a couple of large books. His name was Alexander Wilson, he said, and in Pittsburgh he had met Lucy's uncle, who mentioned Audubon to him as a man interested in birds. The books he carried were the first two volumes of his *American Ornithology*, in which he was describing, in paintings and words, the country's birds. Would Audubon be interested in buying the series? He offered his books.

Snowy Owl. 1829.

This painting, suggestive and magical, is the only night scene in

***The Birds of America*. Audubon once watched a snowy owl catching fish**

at a river and spearing them "like lightning."

It might have been fate, not Audubon's hands, that turned the pages of those books. Certainly it is a remarkable coincidence that two men with the same grand purpose should have met in a backwoods store on the rim of a western wilderness. For Alexander Wilson, an emigrant from Scotland, was doing what Audubon, the transplanted Frenchman, was destined to do: to paint the birds of the country that they both loved deeply.

The urge to draw birds is an ancient one in humans. Eighteen thousand years ago, tribal artists were scratching images of birds on the walls of the caves they lived in. Pictures of birds were used in the hieroglyphic writings of ancient civilizations, and paintings in the tombs of Egyptian pharaohs were alive with ducks and herons and storks. Medieval monks decorated the pages of religious manuscripts with doves and nightingales, and in the sixteenth century illustrated ornithologies became best-sellers.

What attracts artists—and many other people—to birds are their beauty, the grace of their flight, and the feeling of freedom they give us. They touch our spirit and link us closely to nature. In Audubon's time, however, most bird paintings conveyed very little of this. They had considerable art but not very much life. All too often, a bird was portrayed perched stiffly on a branch, looking as stuffed as the specimen it was drawn from. Rarely was there much natural background to enliven the scene or indicate the bird's natural setting. The best of these paintings were done by Chinese artists, who as long ago as the twelfth century were portraying birds with both fidelity and feeling as part of delicate landscapes.

How American birds helped liberate this ancient art takes a little explaining. As they opened up the New World, the explorers brought back a multitude of new species of plants and animals to the naturalists of Europe. Scientists and collectors were avid for specimens, and artists were eager to draw them. Soon men were sent over just to find and gather new species. Mark Catesby, an Englishman who came to America in the early 1700s, journeyed for years through the South collecting and drawing birds and plants. Like so many naturalists, he was an adventurous man. He lived with the Indians and once, without knowing it until he woke up, he shared his bed with a rattlesnake which had crawled in beside him to keep warm. Catesby went back to England to publish his paintings. To save the work and expense of making separate printing plates for plants and birds, he combined them on the same plate, using the plants as background for birds. This practicality crammed each painting with botanical and ornithological details. It also gave a lovely quality to his work and helped introduce a new style in bird paintings.

Somewhat later in the eighteenth century, an American with a similar spirit of adventure made important contributions to ornithology. William Bartram of Philadelphia traveled for years at a time, exploring his country's natural history. Some of his bird paintings have an animation uncommon in the work of the time.

Bartram was a friend and guide to Alexander Wilson, who had come to America in 1794 from Scotland, where he had been a silk weaver and a well-known poet. While making a living as a schoolteacher near Philadelphia, he taught himself to know the native birds and to paint

them—and then determined to publish them in the first American ornithology. When he walked into Audubon's store, he was on one of the many long journeys that would take him from Maine to Louisiana, selling his books.

Audubon was accustomed to the arrival of peddlers offering their wares. Wilson was a very different kind of peddler, and what he was selling fascinated Audubon. He was about to subscribe when his partner, Rozier, spoke to him in French, thinking Wilson would not understand. "Your drawings are far better," he said. Wilson, an educated man, did understand the remark and asked to see Audubon's drawings. Some of them, he said, were quite good.

What Wilson saw were not the Audubon paintings that we know today. Audubon was a ruthless critic of himself. Periodically, often on his birthday, he would go through his collection of drawings and tear up or burn those he thought were not good enough to keep. The ones he kept were often redone or even cut out and pasted up as part of a new painting.

Those drawings that survive intact reveal an artist who had progressed steadily in both his knowledge of birds and his ability to

Arctic Tern. **1833.**

In its tension and simple, dramatic background, this work is

a fine example of Audubon's last great period. The bird was painted on

shipboard off Nova Scotia, then cut out and pasted against a painted sky.

"Light as a sylph," the artist wrote, the tern "dances through

the air" in "beautiful gambols."

depict them but who was just beginning to put a real sense of life into his subjects. By now Audubon was also learning to make artful use of plants. From the start, his drawings had the virtue of being true to nature since he painted from sketches made in the field and from birds he had shot and taken home.

Wilson's visit left a profound mark on Audubon, deeper than he could have realized at the time. Wilson was self-taught in both art and science. So was Audubon. Wilson drew, as Audubon expressed it, "from animated nature" against natural backgrounds. So did Audubon. Yet Audubon knew that what Rozier had said was right: his drawings *were* better than Wilson's. Wilson was accurate and gave his work a stiff, poetic beauty. But Audubon had a grace and understanding that Wilson could never match.

If Wilson could publish his work, Audubon thought, why couldn't he? But he did not follow through on that thought until years later when bad fortune had made a shambles of his life.

Carolina Parakeet. 1825.

In the 1820s Audubon suddenly matured as an artist and entered his rich second period. This is a prime example of his development, a complicated composition showing seven parakeets feeding on cockleburs. "I spared not my labour," the artist said. Once plentiful, the Carolina parakeet has become extinct.

Chapter Four

A
GRAND
AMBITION

The year after Wilson's visit, Rozier and Audubon broke up their partnership. Audubon took over as sole proprietor of their store, which they had moved downriver from Louisville to the smaller town of Henderson, Kentucky. Rozier went off to open his own store and to become a very wealthy man. Audubon should have done well on his own but he was pulled too many other ways—by the wilderness, by his family, and, of course, by birds.

His business, Audubon himself admitted, "went on prosperously when I attended to it. But birds were birds and my thoughts were ever and anon turning towards them as to my greatest delight. Beyond this, I really cared not. I seldom passed a day without drawing a bird or noting something respecting its habits."

Lucy had come to accept the large part of his life her husband gave to birds. "If I were jealous," she once wrote her sisters, "I would have a bitter time of it, for every bird is my rival." Still, she was content. Income from the store kept them comfortable. They bought a sizable log cabin and Lucy filled its shelves with her library of 150 books. They had horses, gardens, and, like everyone who could afford them, three or four slaves to help with the household and the store.

At first Lucy's eastern manners had made her seem snobbish to the other settlers but her good sense and sincerity soon brought her many friends. She was a tough and sturdy woman, as frontier wives had to be. Once, with Audubon, she rode eight hundred miles on Barro to visit her

Always sketching birds and making notes on them, Audubon drew a loon in the journal he kept on his 1820 journey to New Orleans.

family in Pennsylvania. She bore four children. Two daughters died when very young but two sons, Victor and John, throve. Their father encouraged them to draw, and years later they were able to help him with his paintings.

The frontier always attracted men with a willingness to take chances and Audubon took some big ones. He put a good deal of his money into building a river steamboat—a daring venture since the first successful steamboat had been built only a few years before. When the project faltered, Audubon sold his share to some men who went off without paying him. One of the men, whom he was suing for fraud, accosted him on the street and, finding Audubon with an injured hand in a sling, started hitting him with a heavy club. With his good hand, Audubon drew his knife and stabbed his attacker. There was a great commotion in town. Friends of the wounded man laid siege to Audubon's home while Audubon's friends formed a bodyguard. Later in court, the judge found Audubon guilty—not, however, of stabbing the man but, the judge said, of failing "to kill that damned rascal." Audubon never did get his money.

In 1819 another bad investment, in a lumber mill, lost Audubon all the money he had left—as well as most of his friends. His creditors had him jailed and he had to swallow his pride and declare himself bankrupt.

This was a terrible time for Audubon. At thirty-four he was a failure in business, his wife and children dependent on a kind cousin for a place to live. He felt he had been betrayed by "the surly looks and cold receptions of those who so shortly before were pleased to call me their friends." Even the birds, by taking him from his work, had betrayed him and he blamed them for his misfortune. Leaving Kentucky, "with only the clothes I wore, my original drawings and my gun," he set out on "the saddest of all my journeys. The birds that enlivened the woods andprairies all my enemies and I turned my eyes from them as if I could have wished that they never existed."

Now began a life of wandering as Audubon tried to find some way of making a living. He had a knack for making portraits of people, able not only to get a resemblance but also convey character. Pretty soon he had as much work as he could do, although some of it was very strange. He would be summoned to a deathbed to make a last likeness of a dying person, and once a father had his child's coffin dug up and opened so that Audubon could do a posthumous portrait. He quickly forgave the birds he had so bitterly blamed for his troubles,and he would stop work for days on a portrait so he could chase down and sketch a bird he had not drawn before.

It was a skimpy life, even though after a while he was making

Wild Turkey. **1825.**

This was the first plate in *The Birds of America* and, as in all the engravings, the bird was shown full size: about 40 by 30 inches.

enough to rent an apartment for his family. When he heard that a new museum in Cincinnati needed a taxidermist he applied to the museum's founder and director, Dr. Daniel Drake, who was a friend of the New York naturalist Dr. Samuel Mitchill and, like him, well-versed in medicine, botany, zoology, and geology. Dr. Drake was the first man of scientific standing to recognize the worth of Audubon's bird painting. He sponsored the first exhibit of Audubon's drawings, pointing out that Audubon had portrayed many birds that Alexander Wilson had omitted from his *American Ornithology*. When a party of naturalists traveling west on a government expedition came through the city, he invited them to the exhibit and they were impressed by what Audubon was doing.

All this gave Audubon more confidence in his own talents. But things were going badly at the museum. Dr. Drake lacked ready money and was far behind in paying salaries. Though Lucy was employed as a teacher, Audubon decided he would have to make a change. This time it was a momentous one. He would give up everything else in order to paint all the birds of America and publish them in a portfolio that would be more complete than Wilson's—and, he was sure, much better.

It was a brave and reckless ambition. He would have to search out and study hundreds of birds, paint them, interest somebody in publishing engravings of the paintings, and then somehow get people to buy them—all on his own. He had no financial resources and no ready audience to support his project. In the big cities where he would have to find a publisher and a public, no one had ever heard of this bankrupt frontier storekeeper who fancied himself an artist and a scientist.

He also had a family to worry about. All through their lives together,

Lucy had to suffer from her husband's unsettled ways—his neglect of business, his financial mistakes, his long absences. When he sometimes seemed too careless of her needs or stayed away too long, she would scold him or turn cold to his affection. For years she was the one who supported the family and often felt the burden was too much. When Audubon was off in some distant place, she would refuse to join him until he had enough money take care of her and the boys.

Audubon would grow anxious at her refusals, then turn angry and write hurtful letters. But he treasured Lucy. "With her, I was always rich," he said—and Lucy knew this. She not only forgave his carelessness and other faults but also gave all her thoughts and energies to his work. When, in the difficult years to come, he grew discouraged and talked of going back into business, she would have none of it. His bird painting was his life and, though she sometimes found it almost too much for her, she made it her life too.

John James Audubon was now, in 1820, thirty-five years old. His only real asset was himself, not just his talent but his marked and attractive personality. After meeting him, one man came away remembering "his glowing angry eyes, an air which told you, whoever you might be, that he was John Audubon and will never be forgotten by anyone who knew or saw him." His manners were always equal to the occasion, whether he was paying compliments to genteel ladies in an elegant city house or exchanging tall stories with profane backwoodsmen in a log tavern. People were taken with the interesting French accent that colored Audubon's English speech. A friend once wrote down the conversation he had with the artist on their first meeting:

"You are a Frenchman?" the friend had said.

"No, sare. Hi emm an Heenglishman," Audubon replied.

"You look like a Frenchman and you speak like one."

"Hi emm an Heenglishman because hi got a Heenglish wife."

Actually, though his accent was strong and his command of grammar not very sure, Audubon wrote clearly and eloquently in English (it always helped, however, when Lucy or an editor went back over his writing to straighten it out). His prose was flowery, in the manner of his time, but his ornithological observations were clear and to the point. Thanks to Lucy's influence, he had read widely and in his letters and journals he would frequently quote Homer, Shakespeare, and Milton. A good country fiddler, he could also play classical music on the flute.

As a storekeeper he had been a good salesman and this talent in later years enabled him to persuade hundreds of men and women who did not know him to buy his paintings. Sometimes careless about practical matters, he never was careless with his art. Painstaking hours went into getting the right shade of color in a tail feather or the exact number of scales on a bird's tiny claw. He was quick enough to sketch a bird in flight and patient enough to fill in every detail when he turned his sketches into elaborate paintings.

He was methodical at work. After shooting a bird and cleaning it, he would wire it into a position he had chosen, and then pin it up against a large sheet of graph paper so he could get everything in scale. Compasses and calipers helped make his measurements accurate. He could work fast and efficiently, in part because he was ambidextrous and could draw with both hands at once, and in part because he was tireless, sitting at his drawing board for hours at a stretch.

Even when he had become mature and sophisticated, Audubon always revealed something of the boy in his adventurousness, his impulsiveness, and his grand dreams. And also, underneath, was the extraordinary self-discipline that enabled him, with almost no formal training, to make himself a master in art and science.

Louisiana Heron. 1832.

"Delicate in form, beautiful in plumage and graceful in its movements,"

Audubon wrote of the Louisiana heron. The lush Florida landscape

was done by George Lehman, who painted backgrounds

for many Audubon scenes.

It was financial failure that brought this out. Once he had decided to become the painter of America's birds, he never gave up, no matter how harshly fortune seemed to turn against him. Disappointment, rejection, loss—nothing could stop this man who for so many years seemed to be dillydallying with his life.

Leaving Lucy to her job as a teacher in Cincinnati, Audubon set out in October 1820 for Louisiana, hoping to gain backing in the prospering capital, New Orleans. He took with him one of the boys he had been instructing in drawing, thirteen-year-old Joseph Mason, who would draw the botanical backgrounds for his paintings.

The journey south did not seem very promising. The clumsy flatboat moved so slowly that Audubon got off and walked along the bank, shooting birds for his drawings and game for food. When the boat got stuck on sandbars, which it frequently did, Audubon had to jump into the cold waters to help push it off. It was a melancholy trip. Unable to pay full fare, he felt like a pauper. When he tried to feed an eagle he had caught and tethered, it drove its sharp beak into his thumb. To cap it all, his drawings were lost along the way, and when he arrived in New Orleans without them a pickpocket stole his wallet. He took small comfort from the fact that there was little money in it.

His luck improved in the city. His bird drawings would not bring him any money now but his portraits of people did. He was soon making enough from them to send Lucy $275 and twenty bird drawings. Then he had a strange encounter with a lady he called "The Fair Incognito." He told Lucy about it in a letter.

"At the corner of a certain street," he wrote, "I was accosted by a female of fine form, her face so heavily veiled that I could not distinguish her features. She addressed me in animated French—'Pray, Monsieur, are you the one sent by the French Academy to draw the birds of America?'

"I answered that I drew them for my pleasure.

"'It's you who draws likenesses so remarkably strong in black chalk?'

"I granted that I took likenesses in that medium.

"'Then call in thirty minutes at Number —— in —— Street.'

"Astonished beyond description, I waited a while, then started my walk."

When he found her at her home, waiting for him at the top of the stairs, Audubon began "to tremble like a leaf." She threw back her veil to reveal "one of the most beautiful faces I ever saw."

"'Have you ever drawn a full figure—naked?'" she asked.

"Had I been shot by a forty-eight pounder through my heart," Audubon wrote, "my power of speech could not have been more suddenly shut off. To her impatient 'Why don't you answer?' I said, 'Yes.'

"'Return in an hour,' she said."

He did and, commanding him to secrecy, she undressed—which made Audubon so nervous that he dropped his pencil. After he had sketched for an hour, she studied the drawing.

"It is like me," she said.

It took several visits to finish the portrait. When it was completed, she signed her own name in a corner, as if she herself had drawn it, and gave Audubon $120 to buy a fine gun.

"Keep my name forever secret," she told him. He begged leave to kiss her hand.

"She extended it freely," Audubon wrote. "We parted."

Audubon never saw her again and he left two questions: Who was the Fair Incognito? And what did Lucy think of his story?

By lucky chance, Audubon's lost drawings were found and returned to him. He was hired as art instructor to Elizabeth Pirrie, a cotton planter's daughter, and spent a few months on the plantation. The bayou country with its luxuriant trees and flowers and its overflowing bird life entranced him and gave new richness to his paintings.

But life on the plantation became difficult. His student was a spoiled young lady. Her father was an alcoholic. Her mother was suspicious that Elizabeth was growing too fond of her teacher and a suitor thought Audubon was flirting with her. Audubon did not take criticism very well and, after a few months, he was fired. The cash that he took back to New Orleans was very welcome, but it was not as important as the new drawings in his portfolio.

In the year since he left Cincinnati, Audubon had painted sixty-two birds. This in itself was a considerable accomplishment, considering all the time he had to spend earning a living. And suddenly, in one of those remarkable surges of creativity that many artists experience, he was making paintings that were a huge step beyond anything he, or anyone else, had done.

He crowded such beauty and life into his work that it was hard to tell where nature ended and art began. Stiffness was replaced by an animation and a natural grace. The colored chalks and pastels he had been using were put aside for watercolors and they gave his birds the freshness they demanded. He was daring in his composition, fitting seven parakeets into one painting, yet getting unity out of the intricate arrangement (see page 35).

Audubon's work in this first great period is filled with the exuberance of an artist finding himself. The course of his life had always been directed by events, by other people's decisions, or by luck, good and bad. Now his resolve to take destiny in his own hands had brought together everything he had known and learned and felt—the understanding of birds he had gained by years of observation and study, the skills at drawing he had acquired by persistent doing and doing over again, and, above all, the love of nature that had possessed him since childhood.

All this was for a later generation to recognize. Times were still hard for Audubon. When in 1821 Lucy and his sons finally joined him in New Orleans, he was so eager to keep them comfortable that he overworked and nearly collapsed. Some encouragement came from a visiting Englishman who admired Audubon's paintings and advised him to go to England to have them published. This was a fine idea, but how could he do it with so little money?

Mockingbird.

1825.

(detail)

After several months, Lucy found a job teaching the daughters of Jane Percy, the widow of a British naval officer. Lucy was a good teacher, strict but affectionate, who taught her pupils not just arithmetic and grammar but music and manners. Neighbors sent

47

Mockingbird. 1825.

Audubon's painting of a rattlesnake raiding a mockingbird's nest for its eggs got

the artist into trouble. Critics said rattlers don't climb trees or have curved fangs.

But he was proved right.

their children for instruction, and soon Lucy was running a little school on the Percy plantation. Visiting there, Audubon was asked by Mrs. Percy to do portraits of her daughters. When she criticized the results, Audubon rudely refused to make any changes and Mrs. Percy told him to leave.

Lucy was in a predicament. She felt her husband's behavior was inexcusable yet she knew how touchy he was that she was the one who supported the family. Still, she could not afford to give up her job, and so Audubon had to leave. He did—angrily—with their older son. But when the two of them fell ill of yellow fever, Lucy left the plantation to nurse them and stubbornly refused to return until Mrs. Percy let her husband come too.

Upon his recovery, Audubon collected his paintings and set out to find a publisher in Philadelphia. "My friends," he wrote, "regarded me as a madman. My wife determined that my genius should prevail." Barro had long since been sold, so he journeyed by foot, by boat, and by hitchhiking on passing carts, earning money by painting street signs and panels for riverboats. In the spring of 1824 he arrived in Philadelphia.

This was Audubon's first big test and it was a formidable one. Philadelphians were proud that their city had been the country's center for natural history since colonial times, and most of the local naturalists looked down their noses at this unknown artist who was trying to push his way in. Audubon's dramatic style, so different from what they were accustomed to, put them off. His birds, they said scornfully, lacked "truth and correctness." One naturalist, George Ord, who had been a friend and collaborator of Alexander Wilson's, was particularly antagonistic because he saw Audubon as a rival to Wilson. He hounded

Audubon unmercifully for years.

Audubon did not help himself by making uncomplimentary remarks about other artists. But his work was simply too good to ignore. The noted portraitist Thomas Sully said that Audubon's paintings "for strength, expression and exquisite resemblance" far exceeded the work of the European masters. An ornithologist named Charles Lucien Bonaparte, a nephew of Napoleon Bonaparte, the late emperor of France, commissioned Audubon to draw a grackle for a supplement to Wilson's *American Ornithology* that he was preparing. So Audubon's first published bird drawing appeared in a work inspired by that traveling artist who had come calling on him years before.

New York was much more receptive to Audubon. His old friend Dr. Mitchill introduced him to members of the leading natural history society, and they elected Audubon a member and published a paper on swallows he had written. Audubon could feel proud that he was now accepted as a naturalist. He had gained recognition and some prestige. Still no publisher was interested in his bird portfolio.

Audubon's trip back to Louisiana was arduous—sleeping on a boat deck wrapped in a buffalo robe, earning his fare by doing quick portraits and his lodging by giving impromptu flute concerts. His deerskin jacket became frayed, his moccasins all but wore out, and his beard grew so long that he was mistaken for a missionary and asked to give the blessing at dinner table. He came back to Lucy, as he wrote, "with rent and wasted clothes and uncut hair." Mrs. Percy, anxious not to lose Lucy, permitted him to stay.

There was a strength now in Audubon that enabled him to throw off the disappointments of the trip. He was forty years old and he knew he did not have too much time left. Nobody in America would publish his paintings. In England, where there were many more publishers, somebody might.

With Lucy's help he found pupils whom he taught drawing, music, French, and swordsmanship. He was a diligent and popular teacher and on Saturday nights he conducted a dancing class in the village. "With my fiddle under my arm," he wrote, "I placed the gentlemen in line. How I toiled before I could get one graceful step or motion. I broke my bow and nearly my violin in my impatience. Next I had the ladies alone. Then I tried both together—pushed one here, another there—all the while singing to myself. At the close I was asked to dance to my own music. This I did until the whole room came down in thunderous applause. Lessons for the young men in fencing came next and I went to bed extremely fatigued."

The fencing lessons aroused the envy of a local fencing master, who spread malicious gossip about Audubon until someone took him aside and told him what a good shot and swordsman Audubon was. That shut him up.

It was a happy time for Audubon—up before dawn to watch birds and bring back specimens and then, after the day's teaching, working on into the night at his drawings. More and more confident of his skills, he created little dramas in his paintings—for example, showing a family of mockingbirds fighting off a snake (see page 48). In a year and a half, Lucy and he saved up two thousand dollars, enough for a passage to England and the last chance to make good on his grand ambition.

Chapter Five

CONQUEST
OF
ENGLAND

He went by way of New Orleans, stopping there to see Vincent Nolte, the man he and Barro had beaten in that horse race years ago. Nolte had become an influential financier (at one point he was a banker to the Pope) and he gave Audubon a letter of introduction to the Rathbone family of Liverpool, whom he had rescued from financial disaster some years before.

When Audubon called on the Rathbones, they welcomed him warmly and were quickly charmed by his ways and by his art. They were Quakers, and Quakers through their faith had a special interest in natural history. Lugging his portfolio to their home, he opened it up to an array of birds such as they had never seen—fierce hawks clutching their prey, handsome kingfishers swallowing little fish, a turkey large as life almost strutting off the page. They turned the sheets over in delight, exclaiming at their liveliness and beauty.

With the Rathbones' help, Audubon staged an exhibit of his work. It was an immediate and huge success. "La, they are beautiful," the ladies said. One viewer was to sum up their enchantment. Here, he wrote, "sport the feathered races of the New World. Their plumages sparkle with nature's own tints; you see them in motion or at rest, in their play and their combats, in their anger fits and their caresses, singing, running, asleep, just awakened, beating the air, skimming the waves or rending one another in their battles . . . a vision of the New World."

Audubon himself seemed an image of that New World and he deliberately made the most of it, acting the role of an American woodsman fresh from the wilderness—a romantic place the Britishers were eagerly reading about in travelers' tales and the novels of James

Fenimore Cooper. In proper England, Audubon went about wearing his buckskin jacket with its long fringes. His hair hung below his ears and people could smell from across the street the bear grease he smeared on it. When a hostess, serving American food to make him feel at home, offered him corn he astonished her by picking it up in his two hands and eating it off the cob— "as if I intended gagging myself with the ear." When he showed his drawings he accompanied them with sounds— cawing for the crow, quacking for the ducks.

Audubon's artistic development is documented in this painting. The stiff, lifeless goshawk (*lower left*) and Cooper's hawk (*right*) were done about 1809. The lively young goshawk (*top*) was painted in 1830. Audubon put them together for *The Birds of America.*

The Rathbones arranged introductions to the aristocrats of England. Before his visit to Lord Stanley, who would one day become prime minister, Audubon worried "about meeting an English gentleman called a lord." To his astonishment, Lord Stanley put the drawings on the floor and got down on his hands and knees to study them, not what Audubon expected of such a personage. The gentleman called a lord subscribed.

Going to see the earl of Morton, who lived in an enormous castle ornamented with lions, Audubon expected to meet "Richard Coeur de Lion." Instead he was greeted by "a small slender man, tottering on hisfeet, weaker than a new hatched partridge, tears almost trickling from his eyes." He and Lady Morton admired the paintings, and she became a good friend of Audubon's, taking drawing lessons from him and giving him advice on how to behave in England. When he was ready to leave for London, she warned him that his frontier getup would not go over well in that sophisticated city. With great reluctance, Audubon finally cut off his long, shiny hair.

After a while, for special occasions, Audubon would wear a formal hat and carry a sword cane. But he complained about having to put on silk stockings and pumps "and all the finery with which I made a popinjay of myself in my youth." Back home

American Robin. 1829.

The robin was a favorite Audubon subject. He made three paintings of them. This is of a pet robin which, Audubon reported, would fly after his master and "kiss" him on the lips.

in the woods, he would take a chunk of roasting bear meat from a camp fire and eat it from a wood chip that served as his plate. Here he was waited upon by servants wearing red and white livery, which made him feel, he told Lucy, "like a herring on a griddle." So he drank more wine than he should have and regretted it the next morning when he had to get up early and start a day's work. "My head is like a hornet's nest," he moaned, and then would brag that he was visited by "persons of the first rank in society. Think of poor Mr. Audubon, lords sending their carriage to Mr. A. to spend days and nights in their hall."

A far more critical and impressive audience was won over. Invited to address the members of the most important scientific societies, Audubon demonstrated how he drew birds—fixing a specimen on wires, bending its legs, wings, and head into a lifelike position, then quickly making his drawing. It must have been like one of those sleight-of-hand tricks he used to perform for his friends at Mill Grove. When his little act was over, Audubon wrote Lucy, the spectators "clapped hands and stamped the floor. I am positively looked on by all the professors and principal people as a very extraordinary man."

When he first came to England, he said, he had "felt dejected, miserably so, my doubts as to how my work would be received . . . conspired to depress me. Now, how different are my sensations, my works praised and admired, and my poor heart is at last relieved from the great anxiety that for so many years agitated it, for I know now that I have not worked in vain."

And yet, for all the praise, Audubon could not find anyone to publish his work. So he decided to do it himself. He went up to Edinburgh to see William Lizars, the finest printer and engraver in Scotland. Entering the shop, Audubon, as he told it, "slowly unbuckled the straps and without uttering a word, turned up a drawing. Mr. Lizars exclaimed, 'My God, I never saw anything like that before!'"

If they were being published today, Audubon's paintings would be reproduced by machines. In Audubon's time, however, everything was done by hand. The painting was given to a craftsman called an engraver who traced the image on a copper plate using a sharp metal tool. Chemicals were applied to make his lines deeper. Then ink was rolled onto the plate and a sheet of paper pressed against it. When the paper was pulled off, the drawing had been transferred to it. The lines were all in black. Color was painted in by hand, each color separately.

It was a laborious and costly process in which the skill of the engraver was of the greatest importance. Some idea of the difference between Audubon's paintings and the engravings on which they were based can be seen on pages 58, 59, 66, and 67 of this book.

Lizars was more than willing to engrave and print *The Birds of America.* The two men worked out what they would do. The publication, or portfolio, would consist of 400 engravings (eventually this number was increased to 435). Each engraving would be very large, printed on a sheet of paper called an elephant folio, 39½ inches by 29½ inches, nearly four times the size of this page. The size of the engravings on the paper varied, but this way every one of Audubon's birds, even eagles and flamingos, would actually be as close as possible to life size.

The *Birds of America* would be issued in separate folios, each folio containing five individual engravings. A folio would cost two guineas, or about $12. The complete portfolio would cost about $1,000. It would not be sold in bookstores but by subscription, rather like the way magazines are sold today. A subscriber would agree to buy all the parts and pay for them as they were issued. Thus Audubon would be assured a steady flow of cash to keep his project going. He hoped to sell 300 subscriptions (he wound up with 176). Audubon would have been flabbergasted at what the engravings sell for today. A single engraving, for which Audubon got $2, brings almost $50,000 and a complete set of *The Birds of America* is valued at about $2 million.

Black-billed Cuckoo. **1822.**

Here, the elaborate background of a magnolia tree in flower was painted by Joseph Mason, a gifted young pupil of Audubon who went with him to New Orleans in 1820 and did many back- grounds for his teacher's birds. The engraving (right) duplicated the remarkable detail.

Audubon was wearing many hats now: as ornithologist he was studying birds, as artist he was painting them, as publisher he was getting their pictures printed. He now took on another job: as traveling salesman, getting people to subscribe to his work. Since the portfolios were costly, he had to interest well-off people. Often he had a letter of introduction to a possible subscriber. If he had no introduction, he might be treated like a common peddler and turned away. He was such a fine salesman, however, that in a brief time, while making his way from Edinburgh to London, he signed up more than thirty subscribers.

London made Audubon apprehensive—feel as if he were going into "the mouth of an immense monster guarded by millions of sharp teeth." The response to his letters of introduction was slow but they finally gained him audiences with people who might help him. Among them was Sir Thomas Lawrence, the famous portraitist, who found Audubon's paintings "very clever indeed."

Just when things were going well, the whole project threatened to fall apart. Lizars was having trouble with his engravers and was not sure he could do the job. By now Audubon was used to hard luck and had learned that he could turn it to his own advantage. Walking down a London street, he passed an engraver's shop run by Robert Havell. He went in. Would Mr. Havell be interested in working on *The Birds of America?* Havell answered that he was too old to take on such a big job. But there was a good engraver named Colnaghi just around the corner. "Come with me," he said. Colnaghi studied the birds and then went to a pile of  en-gravings, picked one up and showed it to Havell. Havell thought it was lovely.

"That's just the man," he said.

"Then send for your son," replied Colnaghi.

Audubon was baffled until Havell explained. He and his son, Robert, had worked together but quarreled, and young Robert had left his father's shop. Now the elder Havell told Audubon he would get his son to engrave one of Audubon's birds as a sample.

A few days later, Audubon saw the sample, was delighted, and took the Havells on.

The arrangement with the Havells not only brought Audubon a first-class engraver but also brought the two Havells back together again. The son did the engravings and the father supervised the hand-coloring. Their work was even better than Lizars' and cost less. Young Havell, a fine artist himself, was very ingenious in helping Audubon arrange his compositions to fit into the folio sheets and in working out backgrounds.

Things did not go without a hitch or two. Even the best engravers make mistakes, and Audubon had to be on the watch for them. Since the paints were applied by hand by many different people, the coloring was uneven, varying from sheet to sheet, and Audubon had to keep a sharp eye on the results. Both Audubon and young Havell had strong wills, and they sometimes disagreed. Several times Havell was ready to quit. But he stayed on and eventually took over all responsibility for the project. The artistic success of the folios is due, in good measure, to him.

Years of tramping through the wilderness had given Audubon great physical stamina and the memory of all those years he had wasted gave him an unbreakable purpose. He needed both, for there were many things for him to do now—finish his paintings on schedule to keep Havell's shop busy, supervise the work, dash off paintings to sell for day-to-day expenses, keep after subscribers. Many who had signed up were slow in paying and others canceled their subscriptions—which meant getting new ones to replace them.

Londoners became accustomed to seeing Audubon walking through the streets, balancing his bulky portfolios on his head because his arms got tired carrying them. Through his introductions and his exhibits—and his woodsman's ways—he had become well known and widely admired, so it was easier to see prospective subscribers now. He even managed to get King George IV to look at his paintings, something the king's chamberlain said would be impossible. Nothing, the chamberlain said, could drag his Highness away from his endless games of cards.

But when the birds were put before him, the king laid aside his cards and spent some time with the paintings. The future queen, Adelaide, was so impressed with them that she subscribed and allowed her name to be used as a patron of the project, which gave a big boost to Audubon's sales talks.

On a trip to France, Audubon landed two more royal subscribers: the reigning monarch, Charles X, and his successor, the duc d'Orleans, who became King Louis Philippe. The distinguished painter François Gérard said, "Monsieur Audubon, you are the king of ornithological painters." The most eminent scientist in France, Georges Cuvier, was moved to eloquence. Audubon's paintings, he declared, were "the greatest monument ever raised by art to nature."

But the doorman at the Louvre was not impressed. When Audubon went to visit that great museum, he was not allowed in because his dress was unsuitable. He was wearing his trapper's fur hat.

Chapter Six

TRIUMPH IN AMERICA

For the next half-dozen years, Audubon's life is a story of travels—from England to Scotland, from England to France, and three times from England to America. By 1829 he had painted only half as many birds as he needed for his complete work and he decided to go back to America to draw more of them. Besides, he had been away from Lucy for three years. Alarming strains had grown between them. Working hard at her teaching, Lucy was deeply unhappy at her husband's long absence. Sometimes he wrote pleading and demanding that she come join him. In the next letter, he would dismiss the idea as impractical. For a while she would not even answer his letters.

Audubon was torn between remorse at staying away for so long and bitterness at what he thought was Lucy's lack of understanding. His arrogance and indecision reflected his own troubled feelings. For all the enthusiasm and optimism he showed, Audubon had a dark side. His journals reveal the despair that often overcame him. "I have the horrors all around me," he wrote, "dreams of sinking and burning ships at night. Fears of failures have ever been my companions."

Even after he arrived in America, he put off going to Lucy, stopping in the East to find birds he had not yet painted. In four productive months he made forty-two drawings and finally started south to Lucy.

Coming down to Louisiana full of fears and guilt, he stepped into a nightmare. An epidemic of yellow fever had broken out in the bayou

A miniature portrait of Lucy Audubon was done in 1835 in London by Frederick Cruikshank. In England she took on the tedious task of transcribing by hand Audubon's text of *Ornithological Biography* for the printer.

country and, when the boat left him off at a dock at midnight, Audubon found himself in a deserted village without any sign of life. He opened the door of an inn: "All was dark and silent. I called and knocked in vain. It was the abode of Death alone!" He went on to another house, then "another—and another. But the living had fled."

Finally, his knock was answered and, borrowing a horse, he rode through the night, losing his way in the forest. It was barely sunrise when he reached the house where Lucy was living. She was sitting at her piano, giving a lesson. "I pronounced her name gently—she saw me—and the next moment I held her in my arms. Tears relieved our hearts, once more we were together."

He took her back to England, stopping in Washington to enjoy a triumph. By now, the reputation he had gained in England and France had impressed Americans. In the capital, he was invited to the White House, where President Andrew Jackson received him, Audubon was proud to say, "with great kindness." At a meal, Audubon ate wild turkey shot in the

Honored and much sought after in England, Audubon was asked to sit for many portraits. This romantic likeness from 1831 is an engraving of a painting by Frederick Cruikshank, the same artist who had painted his wife.

woods nearby while the president, who had lost his teeth, had bread and milk.

Congress voted to buy a subscription to *The Birds of America,* as much because of patriotism—the birds were all American—as because they appreciated its artistic quality. In 1812 Audubon had become an American citizen and he had deep feelings for his adopted land. On the seal he used to stamp his letters he inscribed the words: "America, My Country."

Problems waited for him when he and Lucy reached London. Fifty subscribers had canceled their orders and he had to acquire others. To add to his burdens, he had undertaken to write what he called an *Ornithological Biography,* five volumes of descriptions of all the birds he painted. He was a very good observer of birds and could depict them in words almost as vividly as he did in paintings. All his writing was done with the help of a Scottish naturalist named William Macgillivray, who edited the manuscripts, and Lucy, who faithfully copied them by hand.

Audubon's description of the courtship of the Canada goose is an amusing example. Picture a gander, he wrote, "who has just accomplished the defeat of another male after a struggle of half an hour or more. He advances gallantly toward the female, his head scarcely raised an inch from the ground, his bill open to its full stretch, his fleshy tongue elevated, his eyes darting fiery glances, and as he moves, he hisses loudly."

At this point, "fierce jealousy urges the defeated gander to renew his efforts to obtain his love. He advances, his eye glowing with the fire of rage, and he hisses with the intensity of anger." The whole flock gathers to view the combat, but the bold gander who won the fight "scarcely deigns to take notice of his foe. He of the mortified feelings, however, raises his body and with a powerful blow sends forth his defiance.

"The affront cannot be borne in the presence of so large a company . . . the blow is returned with vigor, the aggressor reels for a moment, but he soon recovers. . . . Thrust and blow succeed each other like the strokes of hammers. . . . Now the mated gander has caught hold of his antagonist's head with his bill . . . he squeezes him with all the energy of rage and at length drives him away and fills the air with cries of exultation."

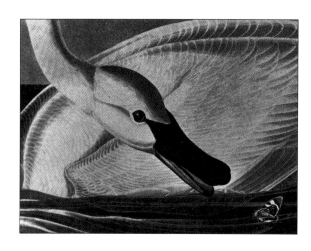

***Trumpeter Swan.* 1837.**

Audubon contorted the trumpeter swan in his painting (right) to fit the folio page. The engraver added a butterfly (see the detail, above), as if the swan was about to eat it. Actually swans seldom eat butterflies.

He witnessed one of the great sights of the bird kingdom, the migratory flight of the passenger pigeon, which once flew in unbelievably huge flocks across North America. "The air," he wrote, "was literally filled with pigeons; the light of noon-day was obscured as by an eclipse." Before sunset the pigeons were still passing in undiminished numbers. They continued to do so for three days. "In these almost solid masses, they darted forward in undulating and angular lines, descended and swept close over the earth with inconceivable velocity, mounted perpendicularly so as to resemble a vast column . . . wheeling and twisting within their continued lines, which then resembled the coils

Passenger Pigeon. 1824.

Passenger pigeons, now extinct, once flew by the millions over the Midwest.
Audubon once watched a flock so thick that, he wrote, the "noonday sun was
obscured as by an eclipse."

Pileated Woodpecker. 1829.

One of Audubon's most popular paintings shows these colorful birds in

an intricate background of wild grape, grabbing worms, pecking a dead elm

for grubs, and chattering at each other.

Chuck-Will's widow
Caprimulgus Carolinensis
Spanish Whip-poor Will common name

72

Blue Jay. 1825. (above)

"Rogues and thieves," Audubon called blue jays, for stealing other birds' eggs.

"Who could imagine that a bird in a garb so resplendent should harbor so much

mischief and malice?" he wrote.

Flamingo. 1838. (left)

In engraving Audubon's birds, Robert Havell often added details not in the original

paintings. For the flamingo engraving, he added a landscape background, some

other flamingos, and drawings of feet taken from the artist's sketchbooks.

Chuck-will's Widow. 1822. (right)

These birds, Audubon wrote, try "to frighten [snakes] away by opening

their prodigious mouths and emitting a strong hissing murmur."

A coral snake appears here.

of a gigantic serpent."

(Nobody in Audubon's time could conceive that a bird so numerous could ever disappear, but the ravages of hunters, who slaughtered them by the tens of thousands, the cutting down of great forests, and other changes in the environment doomed the bird. Within a century after Audubon saw those millions of birds, not a one was left alive.)

To add to all his other concerns, Audubon was still caught up in long and tedious quarrels fomented by George Ord, the friend of Alexander Wilson's who had given Audubon a hard time in Philadelphia years before. Ord accused Audubon of copying Wilson's paintings and passing the copies off as his own. He charged him with scientific falsehood by having shown a rattlesnake climbing up a tree to eat the eggs in a mockingbird's nest—those snakes don't climb trees, Ord insisted. He attacked Audubon's statement that a vulture finds its prey through its sense of sight rather than its sense of smell.

But Ord's accusations did not really stand up. Audubon, in his haste, did copy three of Wilson's drawings, but this transgression is of small significance in view of the hundreds of paintings that flowed from his own brush and the fact that naturalists always borrow from each other. Audubon had not made a mistake in showing a rattler climbing a tree. As for the vulture, it uses both smell and sight, so both Audubon and Ord were right.

In the end, Ord had to surrender. When later on Audubon stopped in Philadelphia, naturalists there ignored Ord's fulminations. They gave Audubon an admiring reception and—the best compliment of all—signed up for The Birds of America.

There was no respite for the artist, chasing after birds from Texas to Florida, where he was almost drowned by a sudden storm, and in 1833 to the Labrador coast, where eighteen-hour working days exhausted him and a rocking schooner kept him constantly queasy. He was out observing and drawing seabirds at three o'clock in the morning, worked until "my fingers could no longer hold my pencil," and was still up at midnight revising the day's work. Once in a while he would quit work early to play his flute for a fisherman's dance.

Others up there were also interested in the nesting birds. "Eggers," they were called. They came to rob birds' nests and sell the eggs in the city markets. A party of four eggers took 40,000 eggs from the nests of geese and a troubled Audubon warned of the day when whole species would be killed off if the practice were not stopped.

Audubon himself killed birds, shooting them to have models for his drawings (and sometimes, after they had served that purpose, eating them for his dinner). Too often, he shot more than he really needed. Today ornithologists rarely shoot wild birds, but times and attitudes were different then. There were so many birds that shooting a few more did not seem to matter. There were not many museum collections for Audubon to study, nor many reference books to consult. He had to build up his own collections of skins and specimens. Only then could he be accurate down to the last necessary detail. His paintings had to be more than works of art; they had to be precise and useful to scientists.

Audubon was not a religious man in any formal sense. But he never ceased to be astonished at the wonderful ways of nature and, like many naturalists, he saw the hand of a Creator in those wonders. As he worked away in Labrador, the land grew bright with flowers and full of birds that had come north on their annual migrations. "In six weeks," he wrote, "I have seen the eggs laid, the birds hatched, their first moult half over, their association in flocks. That the Creator should have commanded millions of delicate, diminutive, tender creatures to cross immense spaces of country to people this desolate land, to enliven it by the songs of the sweet feathered musicians, and by the same command induce them to abandon it almost suddenly is as wonderful as it is beautiful."

The Labrador paintings are a climax to a second great period of Audubon's art. Some of the exuberance of the earlier period has gone but in its place is a mature mastery, a control of his subjects, whether at their ease or in highly dramatic attitudes. He had a sure use of color whether flashing and bright as in the pileated woodpecker (page 73), or subdued and monochrome as in the chuck-will's widow (page 72), or just blue and white as in the blue jay (page 71). There is a classical, almost abstract, beauty in some of his paintings, for example, the trumpeter swan (see pages 66-68).

After Labrador, it was back to England in 1834 to throw together in great haste the last of the bird engravings. For the first time, several species of birds were put together in a single plate. Most of these were birds Audubon himself had not seen, as he put it, "in nature" but had done from specimens other naturalists had lent him. He found some time to enjoy the honors that came easily to him now and to get more subscribers, which did not always come easily. He had particular trouble with the wealthiest banker in Europe, who proved to be very tight with his money. When Audubon called on Baron Rothschild, he found a very fat man who kept hitching up his sagging trousers and spoke brusquely: "I expect you are the publisher of some book or other," he barked. "You may send in your work and I will pay for it."

When he got the bill, the Baron was irate. "What, a hundred pounds for birds?" he cried. "I will give you five pounds and nothing more." Audubon was not going to bargain with the baron and took his engravings back. The tactic worked. Rothschild, who knew fine art when he saw it, gave in and bought the portfolio at Audubon's price.

In 1838 Audubon finished his prodigious work and the next year said his farewell to England. He was grateful to that country, which he had once hated, for having recognized his genius when the country he had adopted ignored him. England gave him a fond send-off. "The American Woodsman's hair had grown quite white," a London newspaper wrote, "his magnificent undertaking is completed. Few have quitted England carrying with them a larger portion of honest regard and sincere good wishes."

Canada Goose. 1833.

Audubon spent days in Maine hunting for a Canada goose, but never saw one. This was drawn from a specimen that a friend gave him.

Chapter Seven

THE LAST ADVENTURE

eady now to stay in America, Audubon published a small, inexpensive octavo edition of *The Birds of America.* Its pages were six inches wide and nine high. The reproductions were done by lithography, a process in which a drawing is made on stone with a special crayon and then transferred to paper. Lithography is both faster and less costly than engraving. The price for the seven volumes of the octavo edition, which also included the text of the *Ornithological Biography,* was $100. For years it was the most complete guide American bird-watchers could buy. It sold remarkably well and Audubon, who had just about broken even on the elephant folio, was at last free of financial worries.

He bought a large plot of land in northern Manhattan along the Hudson River, built a house there, and called it Minnie's Land for Lucy, whose family nickname was Minnie. Believing his wilderness wanderings were over, he tried to bring the wilderness to him. A visitor found "graceful fawns and a noble elk stalking in the shade of the trees." In Audubon's studio, as cluttered as his room at Mill Grove had been, "antlers of elks hung upon the walls, stuffed birds of every description ornamented the mantel, and exquisite drawings of field mice, orioles, and woodpeckers were scattered promiscuously."

There was another grand project in his mind. On one of his trips

Swift Fox.

"A beautiful animal," wrote Audubon of the Swift fox, and he took one back from the west to live in a small menagerie at Minnie's Land in northern Manhattan, where he spent his last years.

south, he had met the Reverend John Bachman of Charleston, South Carolina. Bachman, a naturalist in his own right, became a dear friend of Audubon, and his two daughters married Audubon's two sons. With Bachman as a collaborator, Audubon proposed to do for America's animals what he had done for its birds. It would be a large work called *The Viviparous Quadrupeds of North America* (*viviparous* describes animals whose offspring are born alive, not hatched from eggs).

With Lucy comfortably settled, with his sons to help him, and with money coming in regularly, Audubon still worked as if he had to earn a living and a reputation. At fifty-seven, he complained that he could not work as hard or walk as far as he used to. But a visitor found "his step as light as that of deer" and the penetrating gray eyes "as restless as the glance of an eagle."

In fact, Audubon was restless. He never had been willing to settle down and he wasn't willing even now. He had never traveled far beyond the Mississippi, and he now proposed to go west and get animal specimens. In 1843 he set out on his last adventure.

It was like old days, going by riverboat, only this time he had two assistants and a taxidermist with him, and it was not on a slow barge but

Jaguar.

This painting is by Audubon's younger son, John Woodhouse, who mainly painted the larger animals for *The Viviparous Quadrupeds of North America* (1849–54). As an animal painter, he was as good as his father. He showed his jaguar about to spring on a victim: "It's hair bristles, its tail waves back and forth and all its powerful limbs quiver with excitement."

a modern river steamboat. There were some Indian squaws aboard and, of course, Audubon made friends with them. When he showed a squaw his drawing of a woodchuck, she ran away in great fright. It looked so real that she thought it was alive and that Audubon had created it by some magic.

At a fur-trading post far up the Missouri River, his hostess was a beautiful Indian princess named Natawista. Audubon, who always had an appreciative eye for a handsome woman, admired her as she rode across the plains, her "magnificent black hair floating like a banner behind her" as she shot wolves from the saddle. Astonished that she spoke French as fluently as she spoke Blackfoot, he called her "a lady of breeding, refined in many ways." She managed to spoil that image for Audubon when she brought him a fine buffalo head to draw. Before handing it over to him, she first broke open the skull so she could eat the brains while

On his western trip during the early 1840s Audubon

was sketched at his camp along the Missouri River by his assistant

Isaac Sprague. Sprague later became one of America's

finest botanical artists.

they were still warm. It bothered Audubon that she "partakes of raw animal food with such evident relish."

His old agility was gone, and this almost cost him his life. On a buffalo hunt, a wounded bull charged him and his companion, John Bell. Their pistol shots merely increased the animal's fury. "His appearance," Audubon recalled later, "was now one to inspire terror. Through my own imprudence, I placed myself directly in front of him and as he advanced I fired at his head and then ran ahead of him, not supposing he was able to overtake me; but turning my head over my shoulder, I saw to my horror Mr. Bull within three feet of me, prepared to give me a taste of his horns. The next instant, Bell shot him directly behind the shoulder blade. He tottered for a moment, with an increased jet of blood from the mouth and nostrils, fell forward on his horns, then rolled over on his side and was dead."

However much he enjoyed the hunt, Audubon was saddened by the mindless slaughter of the buffalo, shot for the sheer pleasure of killing them. "What a terrible destruction of life as it were for nothing or next to it, the flesh left to rot. The prairies are literally covered with the skulls of the victims. This cannot last. Even before many years, the buffalo will have disappeared." He was sadly right, of course.

As he set out for home, Audubon carried with him a last memory of the wilderness: "bulls roaring like the continued roll of a hundred drums, elks whistling, wolves howling all around and owls hooting." He was still hardy enough to sleep out on the boat deck on a pile of furs. An admiring young man on board described "his patriarchal beard and hawklike eyes" and thought he was "like one of his old eagles, feathered to the heel."

From the deck, Audubon saw a small animal on a fence some distance away. "See yonder is a fox squirrel," he told his young friend. How could he tell with the animal so far away? "Ah, I have an Indian's eye."

Though his last adventure had left him truly tired, Audubon was soon back in the studio, painting with all his old skill. Though his animals are less spectacular than his birds, they are still superb nature paintings, full of life and truth. *The Viviparous Quadrupeds of North America* consisted of 150 large plates, each 22 by 28 inches, done by lithography. The text for it was written by Bachman.

Age was finally catching up with the artist. He no longer worked so strenuously. His older son, Victor, painted backgrounds for the animals. The younger one, John, was now a first-rate nature artist and painted half of the animals on his own. Audubon would willingly put down his pencil and brush to talk with old friends who came to reminisce, and to

Pine Marten.

"This little prowler," said the text for *Quadrupeds* of the marten, combines "the cunning character of the fox, the cautious habits of the weasel, the voracity of the mink."

receive young naturalists who came to pay homage. He was patron and counselor to a new generation of scientists who were opening up the modern era of American ornithology.

Gently, he slipped into the past, living in his memories, listening to Lucy play the songs he had known as a boy in France and the tunes he had fiddled for the Indians around the campfires. He was sixty-five years old when he died, on January 27, 1851, recalling in his last words the birds he used to stalk in those long-ago days on the young frontier.

Wood Rat.

Western travelers and trappers found the wood rat a pest. It ate

their books, stole their shiny knives and axes, and gnawed at their blankets

in the middle of the night.

Lucy stayed on at their home for a while and ran a small private school. One of her pupils was a boy named George Bird Grinnell, who grew up in a house his family had bought at Minnie's Land. From her he learned about the birds her husband had known and painted.

A last likeness of Audubon was made in the New York photographic studio of Matthew Brady in 1850. His hair is gray, his mouth toothless, but his eyes are still strong and piercing.

Years later, concerned about the alarming rate at which America's birds were being killed, Grinnell founded an organization dedicated to teaching Americans about their birds and to protecting them. He named it the Audubon Society, and there was so much magic in the name—and the cause—that tens of thousands of people who knew about birds through Audubon's paintings and writings rushed to join. Soon Audubon societies were formed in many states and out of them came the National Audubon Society.

The fight to protect birds from hunters who killed them for their plumage or for unrestrained sport was long and difficult. Poachers murdered the Audubon Society's wardens. Politicians derided its efforts. But like their namesake, the Audubon Society never gave up and, in the end, triumphed. Wild birds today are protected by national law and international treaty. More than that, the Audubon societies set an example for the organizations that have been formed to protect all nature and the environment.

This is just one of the many memorials to John James Aubudon. For decades during the nineteenth century, his writings offered the most complete first-hand reporting on America's birds and they are still a treasury of ornithological observation. His paintings have been reproduced in dozens of popular books, and the bird portraits he drew are the best-known images of America's birds.

Sometimes critics today find fault with Audubon's paintings. They contain ornithological inaccuracies, they say, and are overdramatic, showing birds in unrealistic attitudes simply to make a more striking painting. Both complaints are reasonable enough in part but do not subtract from Audubon's whole achievement.

Similar strength in old age is shown below in the photograph of Lucy by Bogardus.

As art, the paintings are unsurpassed. Bold colors are used freely but they never clash: they support each other. The compositions hold together even though they are filled with detail. Audubon made himself a master of detail. The scales on a bird's foot become an artful design; the feathers on a breast have a softness that can almost be felt.

Audubon gave his paintings an all-important, unifying point of view. This has been explained by Robert Welker in his book *Birds and Men*. In Audubon's paintings, he says, the bird "is not moved into place for the observer but the other way around. We are at ground level to see two black vultures squabbling over the head of a deer; we peer through blackberry brambles to see the towhee. We find ourselves far up in a black walnut tree to look at a crow and we fly hundreds of feet above earth and water with the golden eagle and the osprey. There is a sense of immediacy, of identification, an intimacy and understanding." At the heart of all of Audubon's work is this intimacy and understanding. It reflects not just Audubon's methods but his most profound feeling.

Audubon was a man with a passion for nature, and he declared this passion to the world through his portraits of the birds he so greatly loved. It is this love for birds and for nature that leaves its deepest mark on us today. Looking at the paintings, we come to understand his love and, in some way, feel it ourselves. This may be the best of all the legacies that John James Audubon has left.

Audubon drew this sketch (left) of himself when he was a vigorous 36-year-old visiting England. He scribbled below it the date and the words "Almost Happy!!"

***Golden Eagle.* 1833. (right) Adding a little story to his painting of a golden eagle clutching a rabbit, Audubon depicted a huntsman—probably himself—crossing a gorge on a log. The figure was left out of the engraving.**

LIST OF ILLUSTRATIONS

Page 58:
Black-billed Cuckoo. 1822. Pencil, watercolor, pastel, and lacquer, 19³/₈ x 24¹/₈". Courtesy The New-York Historical Society, New York

Page 59:
Robert Havell and Son. *Black-billed Cuckoo.* Engraving. Courtesy The New-York Historical Society, New York

Page 62:
Frederick Cruikshank. *Portrait of Mrs. Audubon.* 1835. Courtesy The New-York Historical Society, New York

Page 64:
Frederick Cruikshank. *Portrait of Audubon.* c. 1831. Painting based on engraving by C. Turner. Courtesy American Museum of Natural History, New York

Page 66:
Trumpeter Swan (detail of engraving).

Pages 67–68:
Trumpeter Swan. c. 1836. Watercolor, 23 x 37⁵/₈". Courtesy The New-York Historical Society, New York

Page 69:
Passenger Pigeon. 1824. Pencil, watercolor, and pastel, 26¹/₈ x 18¹/₄". Courtesy The New-York Historical Society, New York

Page 70:
Flamingo. 1838. Watercolor, 33 x 24". Courtesy The New-York Historical Society, New York

Page 71:
Blue Jay. 1825. Watercolor, pencil, and ink, 23¹/₂ x 18³/₄". Courtesy The New-York Historical Society, New York

Page 72:
Chuck-will's Widow. 1822. Watercolor, 23¹/₂ x 18⁵/₈". Courtesy The New-York Historical Society, New York

Page 73:
Pileated Woodpecker. 1829. Watercolor, ink, and lacquer, 37³/₄ x 25¹/₈". Courtesy The New-York Historical Society, New York

Page 77:
Canada Goose (detail). 1821/33. Watercolor, 38¹/₈ x 25³/₄". Courtesy The New-York Historical Society, New York

Page 78:
Swift Fox. 1851. Engraving by Trembly after J. W. Audubon, 6¹/₂ x 10³/₈".Courtesy The New-York Historical Society, New York

Page 81:
The Jaguar. 1854. Engraving by W. E. Hitchcock after J. W. Audubon, 6¹/₂ x 10³/₈". Courtesy The New-York Historical Society, New York

Page 82:
Isaac Sprague. *Encampment of J. J. Audubon and Party.* 1843. Pencil. Courtesy American Museum of Natural History, New York

Page 84:
Pine Marten. 1854. Engraving by W. E. Hitchcock after J. W. Audubon, 6¹/₂ x 10³/₈". Courtesy The New-York Historical Society, New York

Page 85:
Wood Rat (Rocky Mountain Neotoma). 1849. Engraving by Trembly after J. W. Audubon, 6¹/₂ x 10³/₈". Courtesy The New-York Historical Society, New York

Page 86:
Matthew Brady. *Portrait of Audubon.* 1850. Daguerreotype. Courtesy The Audubon Museum, Henderson, Kentucky

Page 87:
Bogardus. *Portrait of Lucy Bakewell.* Photograph. Courtesy The New-York Historical Society, New York

Page 88:
Self-Portrait. 1826. Pencil and charcoal, 5⁵/₈ x 4¹/₄". Richard R. Rathbone Collection

Page 89:
Golden Eagle. 1833. Watercolor, 38¹/₈ x 25¹/₂". Courtesy The New-York Historical Society, New York

Photograph Credits:
Courtesy Department of Library Services, American Museum of Natural History, New York: pages 2–3, 6 (photo by Logan), 8, 10, 21, 62, 82; Courtesy Douglas Kenyon, Inc., Chicago: 86; © President and Fellows of Harvard College: 26

INDEX